FESTIVE FOODS
UNITED STATES

Sylvia Goulding

CHELSEA CLUBHOUSE

An Imprint of Chelsea House Publishers

Copyright © 2008 The Brown Reference Group plc.

Chelsea Clubhouse
An imprint of Chelsea House Publishers
132 West 31st Street
New York, NY 10001

Library of Congress Cataloging-in-Publication Data

Goulding, Sylvia.
  Festive foods / Sylvia Goulding. – 1st ed.
    v. cm.
  Includes bibliographical references and index.
  Contents: [1] China – [2] France – [3] Germany – [4] India – [5] Italy – [6] Japan – [7] Mexico – [8] United States.
  ISBN 978-0-7910-9751-9 (v. 1) – ISBN 978-0-7910-9752-6 (v. 2) – ISBN 978-0-7910-9756-4 (v. 3) – ISBN 978-0-7910-9757-1 (v. 4) – ISBN 978-0-7910-9753-3 (v. 5) – ISBN 978-0-7910-9754-0 (v. 6) – ISBN 978-0-7910-9755-7 (v. 7) – ISBN 978-0-7910-9758-8 (v. 8)
  1. Cookery, International. 2. Gardening. 3. Manners and customs. I. Title.
  TX725.A1G56 2008
  641.59–dc22
                    2007042722

Chelsea Clubhouse books are available at special discounts when purchased in bulk quantities for businesses, associations, institutions, or sales promotions. Please call our Special Sales Department in New York at (212) 967-8800 or (800) 322-8755.

You can find Chelsea Clubhouse on the World Wide Web at
http://www.chelseahouse.com

Printed and bound in Dubai

10 9 8 7 6 5 4 3 2 1

For The Brown Reference Group plc.:
Project Editor: Sylvia Goulding
Cooking Editor: Angelika Ilies
Contributors: Jacqueline Fortey, Sylvia Goulding
Photographers: Klaus Arras, Emanuelle Morgan, Dirk Scholz
Cartographer: Darren Awuah
Art Editor: Paula Keogh
Illustrator: Jo Gracie
Picture Researcher: Mike Goulding
Managing Editor: Bridget Giles
Production Director: Alastair Gourlay
Editorial Director: Lindsey Lowe
Children's Publisher: Anne O'Daly

Photographic Credits:
Front Cover: Klaus Arras
Back Cover: Klaus Arras
Alamy: Goss Images 30; **Fotolia:** 4, 6, 18, 44; **istock:** title page, 3, 5, 15, 17, 24, 26; **Shutterstock:** 3, 5, 7, 8, 9, 10, 12, 13, 20, 22, 23, 25, 28, 31, 34, 35, 36, 38, 39, 41

With thanks to models:
Anouk, Bundhalee, Fidan, Florian, Malcolm

Cooking Editor
Angelika Ilies has always been interested in cookery and other countries. She studied nutritional sciences in college. She has lived in the United States, England, and Germany. She has also traveled extensively and collected international recipes on her journeys. Angelika has written more than 70 cookbooks and cooking card series. She currently lives in Frankfurt, Germany, with her two children and has spent much time researching children's nutrition. Both children regularly cook with their mother.

Contents

let's
START COOKING

Cooking is fun—you learn about different ingredients and cooking methods, you find out how things taste, and you can serve a meal to your family and friends that you have cooked yourself! Some of the recipes in this book have steps that need adult help—ask a parent or other adult if they will be your kitchen assistant while you cook a meal.

This line tells you how many people the meal will feed.

In this box, you find out which ingredients you need for your meal.

WHAT YOU NEED:

SERVES 4 PEOPLE:

2¼ cups white rice
4 eggs, beaten
light soy sauce
4 tablespoons
    groundnut
    or soy oil
2 green onions
⅓ cup peeled shrimps
⅓ cup ham
⅓ cup green peas

Check before you start that you have everything you need. Get all the ingredients ready before you start cooking.

◁ I always help in the kitchen. Cooking a meal is great fun. You also find out what people around the world eat every day and for special celebrations.

! WHEN TO GET help

Most cooking involves cutting ingredients and heating them in some way, whether frying, boiling, or cooking in the oven. Each time you see this exclamation mark, be extra careful as you cook and make sure your adult kitchen assistant is around to help.

For many meals you need to chop an onion. First cut off a thin slice at both ends. Pull off the peel. Cut the onion in half from end to end. Put one half with the cut side down on the chopping board. Hold it with one hand and cut end-to-end slices with the other hand. Hold the slices together and cut across the slices to make small cubes. Make sure you do not cut yourself!

Other recipes in this book use fresh chilies. Always wear rubber or surgical gloves when chopping chilies. If you don't have any gloves, wash your hands very thoroughly afterward, and do not touch your skin for a while. Chili seeds and the white pith contain a substance that makes your skin burn. Trim off the stalk and halve the chili lengthways. Scrape out the seeds and throw them away.

Measuring cups help you figure out how much of a particular ingredient to use. Sets may include ⅛, ¼, ⅓, ½, ⅔, ¾, and 1-cup measures.

A **wire whisk** is good for whisking egg whites or egg yolks. You can also whisk other ingredients together to make a liquid mixture.

Oven gloves or mitts are essential in any kitchen. Wear them each time you touch a hot dish from the oven or the stove, or if you need to stir something.

A **rolling pin** is a useful kitchen tool for rolling out the dough on the board if you are making cakes, breads, pies, pastry, or cookies.

A trip around the
UNITED STATES

The United States stretches from coast to coast between the Pacific and Atlantic oceans. Its land area makes it the world's third-largest country.

The United States is so large, it takes five days to travel from one side of the country to the other by car. On such a journey you cross four time zones: Eastern, Central, Mountain, and Pacific time. Forty-eight states are grouped together, and two are separated from the rest. Alaska, the largest, forms the upper western section of the North American continent. The volcanic islands of Hawaii lie in the Pacific Ocean.

The northern border with Canada is the world's longest continuous border. It runs from Washington State in the west to Maine in the northeast. The border passes through mountains, forests, prairies, lakes, and Niagara Falls. The country's southern border with Mexico crosses four U.S. states.

The Mississippi–Missouri River is 3,740 miles long and the fourth longest river in the world. It runs from the north to the south. The Great Lakes in the north are the world's largest group of freshwater lakes.

The East

The Atlantic coastal plain stretches from Maine down to Texas. Farther west, the Appalachian mountain belt sweeps from New York State to Alabama. Settlers arrived on the

◁ **The United States** has a population of 302,254,000 people. They are of many different ethnic origins. The majority are Anglo-Americans. Other large ethnic groups are Hispanics, African Americans, and Asian Americans.

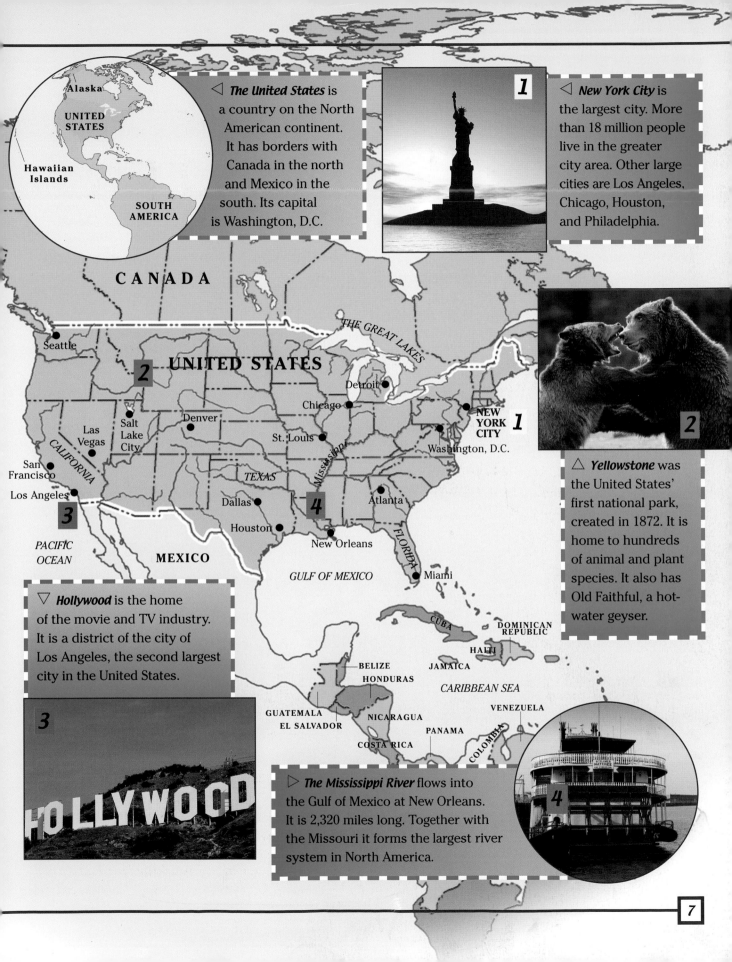

The United States is a country on the North American continent. It has borders with Canada in the north and Mexico in the south. Its capital is Washington, D.C.

1

◁ **New York City** is the largest city. More than 18 million people live in the greater city area. Other large cities are Los Angeles, Chicago, Houston, and Philadelphia.

Alaska

UNITED STATES

Hawaiian Islands

SOUTH AMERICA

CANADA

Seattle

THE GREAT LAKES

2 UNITED STATES

Detroit

Chicago

Denver

Salt Lake City

St. Louis

NEW YORK CITY

1

Las Vegas

CALIFORNIA

San Francisco

Los Angeles

3

TEXAS

Mississippi

Dallas

Houston

4

Atlanta

Washington, D.C.

New Orleans

FLORIDA

Miami

2

△ **Yellowstone** was the United States' first national park, created in 1872. It is home to hundreds of animal and plant species. It also has Old Faithful, a hot-water geyser.

PACIFIC OCEAN

MEXICO

GULF OF MEXICO

▽ **Hollywood** is the home of the movie and TV industry. It is a district of the city of Los Angeles, the second largest city in the United States.

CUBA

DOMINICAN REPUBLIC

HAITI

BELIZE

HONDURAS

JAMAICA

CARIBBEAN SEA

3

GUATEMALA

EL SALVADOR

NICARAGUA

COSTA RICA

PANAMA

VENEZUELA

COLOMBIA

HOLLYWOOD

▷ **The Mississippi River** flows into the Gulf of Mexico at New Orleans. It is 2,320 miles long. Together with the Missouri it forms the largest river system in North America.

4

eastern coast in the seventeenth century. Most people in the east now live in the large cities (Boston, New York, Philadelphia, and Washington). The cities have skyscrapers in the center and sprawling suburbs.

The capital is Washington, D.C. The northeastern states, such as Vermont, have an attractive rolling landscape. Along the coast there are river inlets, islands, natural harbors, fishing villages, and lighthouses.

The Southeast and South

The southern coastal plain contains marshy areas called wetlands. These include the Great Dismal Swamp in Virginia and North Carolina, the bayous of Louisiana, and the Everglades in Florida. Florida juts out into the sea. It has the Atlantic Ocean to the east and the Gulf of Mexico to the west.

Its warm climate makes Florida a popular state to live in. The cities of Miami (Florida), New Orleans (Louisiana), and Houston (Texas) are on the Gulf of Mexico. The Rio Grande and the Mississippi River flow into the Gulf of Mexico.

▽ *Plantation homes* still stand in Louisiana and other southern states. They tell the story of rich landowners and their slaves. The houses are built in the colonial style. Many are now museums.

In the southern states of Alabama, Mississippi, and Louisiana, landowners grew cotton on large plantations. Slaves were brought from Africa to work there. After a long and painful struggle, they were freed and became the ancestors of many of today's African Americans.

The Midwest

The five Great Lakes—Superior, Michigan, Huron, Erie, and Ontario—are in the northern center. Ships still carry goods on their waters. They are linked to the sea by the St. Lawrence Seaway. The industrial cities of Chicago and Detroit grew up as inland ports. The land south of the lakes is rich and fertile. Farther west, the Great Plains extend down the center of the United States from north to south.

The West

The Rocky Mountains form a broad backbone, 3,000 miles long. They pass through eleven states, from beyond the Canadian border

△ **The Grand Canyon** is a steep, colorful valley cut into the rocks by the Colorado River in Arizona. The canyon is 227 miles long, and in some places it is more than a mile deep.

down to New Mexico. Rushing rivers flow from their snowcapped peaks. The Cascade Mountains in the northwest have volcanoes, including Mt. Rainier and Mt. St. Helens.

Farther south, the state of California has its own spectacular mountain range, the Sierra Nevada. San Francisco and Los Angeles are the largest cities in California. Here the weather is warm all year round. In the drier southwest, there are deserts. These include Death Valley, the hottest place on Earth (134°F). Nearby is the great valley of the Grand Canyon.

Native American tribes of Navajo, Hope, Zuni, and Apache people live in reservations in the southwest. Many people cross the southern border from Mexico into the United States seeking work. Spanish is often spoken here.

The food we grow in the
UNITED STATES

The United States enjoys a moderate climate. It has fertile soil, as well as long coastlines and waterways.

Wheat and other grains, corn, fruit, and vegetables are the main foodstuffs that grow in the United States. Beef, pork, and poultry are raised here, and fish and seafood are caught off the long coastlines.

The Midwest

People call the Midwest the "breadbasket" of the United States. The natural landscape was once a type of grassland, called a prairie. Early settlers from Europe discovered that cereal plants grow well in its fertile soil. Today, millions of tons of wheat, oats, and corn are produced each year.

The Corn Belt stretches across the center of the United States. It includes the states of Iowa, Nebraska, Illinois, Minnesota, and Indiana. Their rich soil, warm weather, and rain are good for growing corn. Corn is also grown in the east and south of the country. Most of the corn feeds farm animals.

After corn, the second biggest crop is soybeans. They are grown in the Midwest and southward along the Mississippi. The states of North Dakota, Montana, Kansas, and

▽ **The Great Plains** are flat. Vast prairies stretch as far as the eye can see. The main features here are isolated farmsteads and silos for grain storage—and long, empty highways.

BEST FOR BUFFALOES

Thousands of settlements on the Great Plains have become ghost towns as people move away. The driest areas may be restored to native grassland so the buffalo can roam freely.

Oklahoma are centers for growing wheat. Wheat is used to make flour for bread, cakes, pasta, and noodles.

Cattle country

Texas is the United States' No. 1 producer of great beef for steak and burgers. Families run most of its farms. Cattle ranching in Texas began when the Spanish introduced cattle nearly 300 years ago. The famous longhorn cattle were kept on large areas of land called ranches. Cattle also roamed freely on rich pastures in open country, known as range.

Cattlemen, or cowboys, drove cattle along trails to the nearest railroad. From there they

△ **Pumpkins** grow throughout much of the United States. They can be made into great jack-o'-lanterns at Halloween. They are also used to make delicious pumpkin butter, pies, bread, pudding, cookies, and soup.

▽ **Shorthorn cattle** are one of the main breeds on farms today. They grow quickly and soon put on weight. They are hardy and don't become sick. And—they have short horns!

Fishing

Fishers set out from New England ports to catch Atlantic cod. There are fewer cod today because of overfishing. On the northwest coast, Alaskan waters net rich catches of salmon, cod, pollock, and crab.

Chesapeake Bay in Virginia is famous for its seafood. In this large river mouth, salt and freshwater mix together, so a rich variety of sealife can live here. Fishers gather clams and oysters, and catch crabs and many kinds of fish. Small fish farms in the South raise catfish and shellfish in ponds. Here seafood is made into tasty gumbo stews and jambalayas.

California

California has about 77,000 farms and ranches. This state is the top producer of fruit and vegetables in the United States. The favorite meals here are healthy salads, as well as grilled and baked vegetables and potatoes. California has warm summers and mild winters, so some foods can be grown all year long.

The large flat Central Valley runs for about 400 miles from north to south through the center of the state. Here farmers produce a fourth of the food eaten in the states. The major foods are almonds, grapes, apricots, asparagus, avocados, lettuce, strawberries, and tomatoes.

The South

The peanuts in our peanut butter probably come from Georgia, Florida, Alabama, the Carolinas, or Texas. Peanut bushes need warm weather to grow well. The nuts ripen underground. Florida is famous for its oranges and other citrus fruit. Its key limes are used to make delicious key lime pies.

△ *Most pineapples* in the United States come from Hawaii. Some are also grown on the island of Puerto Rico. Other tropical fruit from these islands include mangoes, pomegranates, bananas, papayas, and avocados.

were sent to northern slaughterhouses. Today, more and more people choose natural beef. It comes from cattle raised without the use of growth hormones or antibiotics.

Texas also raises more sheep than any other state. Flocks of sheep roam the ranges of the western United States, in states such as California, Wyoming, and Colorado.

let's make...
BAKED POTATOES

This dish is not only easy to make, it's also packed with goodness. Potatoes have loads of fiber and vitamins. They're also low-fat. Of course, that all depends on your toppings...

▽ The great thing about baked potatoes is that you can come up with endless ideas for fillings.

WHAT YOU NEED:

SERVES 4 PEOPLE:

4 large starchy potatoes,
   all about the same size
cooking oil
4 tablespoons butter
salt, black pepper
½ cup sour cream
   or crème fraîche
2 egg yolks
fresh chives

WHAT'S THIS: starchy potato?

These potatoes have lots of starch but little moisture. They turn fluffy after baking. The best type is the russet or Idaho potato.

MY TIP

Try making this dish with a sweet potato for a change.

1 Heat the oven to 400°F. Thoroughly wash and brush the potatoes. Brush them all over with oil. Place the potatoes on a rack and bake in the oven for 1 hour.

!

2 Allow the potatoes to cool a little. Cut a "lid" from each potato. Carefully hollow the potato out with a spoon, leaving a ½-inch edge.

3 In a bowl, mash the potato flesh with a fork. Stir in 3 tablespoons butter and allow this to melt. Season the purée with salt and pepper.

4 In another bowl, stir together the sour cream with the egg yolks. Stir this mixture into the purée.

6 Wash the chives, snip with scissors into short ends. Sprinkle them over the potatoes and serve.

5 Fill the hollow potato shells with the mixture. Place the potatoes side by side in a shallow ovenproof dish. Dot each one with the rest of the butter and bake the potatoes for another 5 minutes.

let's make...
JAMBALAYA

Jambalaya is a favorite rice dish in the Southern States. The basics are rice, tomatoes, and lots of spices. Then we add shrimps, chicken, ham, or salami.

WHAT YOU NEED:

SERVES 4 PEOPLE:

salt, black pepper
1 cup short-grain rice
2 onions
1 garlic clove
2 chilies
3 sticks celery
1 bell pepper

1 bunch flat-leaved parsley
3 tablespoons butter
1 small can peeled tomatoes
(8 ounces)
1 tablespoon tomato purée
1 pinch ground cloves
Cayenne pepper

FOR THE SAUCE:

8 ounces ham
(1 slice as thick
as a finger)
1¼ cups shelled
shrimps

◁ Every time Mom cooks a meal, I hope she cooks more than we can eat! All the tasty leftovers end up in the next Jambalaya—ham and shrimps are best!

WHAT'S THIS: Jambalaya?

There are Creole and Cajun Jambalayas. Our recipe is for a quick Creole version. This one-pot dish was made by Europeans who settled in the French Quarter of New Orleans. They wanted to make paella but had no saffron. Over the years it became a quite different dish, with tomatoes and Caribbean spices.

1 In a saucepan, bring 4½ cups lightly salted water to a boil. Sprinkle in the rice, cover, and simmer over low heat for 20 minutes.

3 Put the butter into a large saucepan, and heat until it foams. Add the onion and fry until it becomes transparent (see-through). Add the garlic, chili, celery, and peppers. Fry and stir gently for a few minutes.

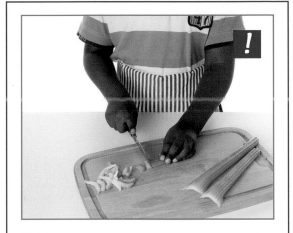

2 Meanwhile, peel and finely chop the onions and the garlic. Deseed chilies and cut them into thin rings *(see page 5)*. Cut the celery into thin slices. Halve and deseed the bell peppers. Cut them into thin strips. Chop the parsley.

4 Add the tomatoes and their juice. Squash them with a spoon. Stir in half the parsley. Season the mix with tomato purée, ground cloves, black pepper, Cayenne pepper, and salt. Simmer over low heat for 5 minutes.

5 Drain the rice. Cut the ham into cubes. Wash the shrimps under cold water. Stir the ham, shrimps, and rice into the tomato sauce. Simmer for 5 more minutes. Sprinkle with the remaining parsley and serve.

let's make...
KEY LIME PIE

This is one of the great recipes from Florida. The "key" in the name comes from Key West, the island at the southern tip of Florida. People grow lots of citrus fruit there.

▽ I call key limes "confused lemons" because they're all yellow like lemons. Persian limes—like the one I'm tasting here—are usually easier to find in the food stores. Limes taste sour if you eat them raw, but key lime pie is sweet!

WHAT YOU NEED:

MAKES 12 SLICES:

1 pastry base (or ready-made pastry crust)

FOR THE CREAM:

1 can sweetened condensed milk (8 ounces)

6 egg yolks
3–4 limes

FOR THE MERINGUE:

6 egg whites
⅞ cup sugar

PLUS:

softened butter for the mold

WHAT'S THIS: <u>key lime?</u>

Key limes are much smaller, rounder, and paler than the limes we find in most markets. And they are extra sour. If you can find them, you'll need more limes—about 12 for one pie.

1 Heat the oven to 400°F. Place the pastry base in a pie dish. Or, if you are using ready-made pastry, roll it out to fit the dish. Prebake the pastry following the packet instructions. **!**

3 Whisk the condensed milk together with the egg yolks until the mix is thick. Stir in the lime zest and juice.

4 Pour the cream onto the pastry base and smooth it. Bake the pie in the bottom of the oven for 25 minutes.

2 Make the cream: Thoroughly wash the limes and grate the zest of 2 limes. Press as many limes as you need to make ½ cup lime juice.

5 Meanwhile, whisk the egg whites until they form a stiff meringue. Drizzle in the sugar as you whisk.

6 When the pie is baked, spread the meringue on top and make a nice pattern. Heat the oven broiler, and cook the pie for 5 minutes until golden. Watch all the time so it doesn't burn. Take out, allow to cool, and decorate.

How we celebrate in the
UNITED STATES

Many Americans celebrate the traditional holidays of New Year, Easter, and Christmas. But there are other holidays that are celebrated only in the states.

*T*he greatest festivals are July 4th, or Independence Day, and Thanksgiving. There are also many regional festivals and celebrations for specific community groups, such as people from an Irish background.

The Fourth of July

On July 4th, the United States celebrates its own birthday. The nation was "born" over 200 years ago, on July 4th, 1776. On this day, Congressmen approved the Declaration of Independence. The United States numbered only thirteen states. They became a new nation, independent of Great Britain.

Today, this day is celebrated with parades and baseball games. At night, there are great fireworks, often in the national colors of red, white, and blue. There is bunting everywhere, and orchestras play patriotic songs such as "The Star-Spangled Banner," "God Bless America," and "America the Beautiful."

Many people spend the holiday with their family and friends. They often have a picnic or a barbecue. Traditional foods to eat on

this day include apple or blueberry pie and ice cream. People grill hamburgers and hot dogs on barbecues at home or in a park. Potato salad, coleslaw, and corn-on-the-cob are popular side dishes. Many people make special red, white, and blue decorations.

Thanksgiving

The first people to celebrate Thanksgiving were the Pilgrim Fathers. They had fled from England, where they were not allowed to practice their religion. They settled in Virginia in the early seventeenth century. Life was hard for the new settlers, and many people did not survive the harsh winter. When they had their first good harvest, they gave thanks to God and celebrated with a feast.

Today, Thanksgiving is an annual holiday on the fourth Thursday in November. Some foods are always eaten during a Thanksgiving dinner. Turkey is all-important but people also have sweet potatoes, yams, corn, and cranberry sauce. The settlers learned about all these foods from Native Americans.

◁ *The Stars and Stripes* fly everywhere on national holidays such as Independence Day. People decorate their homes, clothes, and even their dogs in red, white, and blue. Some people also paint their faces in the national colors.

PARDON ME

Each year, the President of the United States "pardons" one turkey (or sometimes two) just before they are to be slaughtered. In recent years, the pardoned birds were flown to Disneyland to end their days there in peace.

Mardi Gras

Mardi Gras or "Fat Tuesday" is the last day and high point of the carnival in New Orleans. It is the day before Ash Wednesday, which is the start of Lent. For two weeks, the town is decorated in purple (said to mean justice), green (for faith), and gold (for power). Many parades are organized by the so-called "krewes," or carnival associations. The best-known krewes are Rex and Zulu. The krewe members throw colorful bead necklaces, dubloons, cups, masks, or other trinkets to parade goers. The spectators are dressed in crazy costumes and try to catch as many throws as possible. People enjoy crawfish stews and street parties or go to balls.

△ *Mardi Gras parades* have large, colorful floats. The krewes all elect a king for the day. Rex krewe's king is King Carnival. His opposite is King Zulu, of the Zulu krewe.

The Chicago River is dyed green to celebrate St. Patrick's Day. It is said that you have to wear green to show your "Irish" colors. Green is also the color of spring and hope, and of the shamrock, symbol of the Holy Trinity.

Martin Luther King's life, work, and dreams are celebrated in January. Reverend King was a civil rights leader. He opposed injustice and inequality and led nonviolent protests.

St. Patrick's Day

Saint Patrick brought Christianity to Ireland. He is Ireland's patron saint. Catholic Irish settlers brought the holiday and its traditions to the United States.

St. Patrick's Day is now a national holiday for Irish people. They celebrate their heritage and tradition—and many non-Irish people join in. There are parades in all the cities where many Irish people live. The parade in New York City is the largest in the world.

Green is the color of the day. People wear green clothes or paint their faces green. Some people decorate their cars and their pets. The towns go one step further. Some mark the traffic stripe on the parade routes with the color green. Chicago dyes its river green, and other cities turn the water in their fountains or canals green. People might even eat all-green foods, such as green salads, avocados, pea soup, lime pudding, and other dishes colored green with food dye.

REV. MARTIN LUTHER KING, JR.
1929 — 1968
"Free at last. Free at last.
Thank God Almighty
I'm Free at last.

let's make...
ROAST TURKEY

For Thanksgiving Day, the whole family gets together and we share a huge turkey. Mom makes a delicious pan gravy to go with it. We also usually eat a roast turkey for Christmas.

▽ All morning, I can smell the turkey roasting. When we sit down together at the table to eat it, it's really hard to wait!

WHAT YOU NEED:

SERVES 6-8 PEOPLE:

1 onion
2 sticks celery
⅓ cup butter
7–8 ounces sausage
   meat (optional)
1 bunch parsley, chopped
1 teaspoon dried thyme

a pinch dried sage
salt, black pepper
10 ounces corn
   or wheat bread
1 cup chicken stock
1 turkey (about 8–10 lbs)
3 tablespoons shortening

FOR THE GRAVY:

1¾ cups chicken
   stock
2 tablespoons
   butter
2 tablespoons
   flour

MY TIP

To test if the turkey is done, insert a toothpick into the thickest part of the leg, then pull it out again. If the juices that run out are clear, the turkey is done. If the juices are pink, it needs to cook for longer.

1 Peel the onion, wash and trim the celery, and cut both into cubes. Heat the butter in a skillet until it foams. Add the vegetables and fry over medium heat for about 5 minutes.

2 Add the sausage meat, if using. Fry and stir for 3–4 more minutes. Season with herbs, salt, and pepper.

3 Cut the bread into bite-sized cubes. Stir it into the vegetable and meat mixture, together with the stock, a bit at a time. The mix should be moist but not runny. Keep some of the bread out if it gets too dry.

4 Wash and pat the turkey dry. Rub it inside and out with salt and pepper. Fill the belly with the bread mixture. Close the opening with toothpicks.

6 Make the gravy. Spoon off some fat from the roasting juices and throw it away. Pour the juices into a saucepan. Stir in the stock. Bring to a boil. Fork together the butter and the flour, then add, a little at a time. Cook for a few minutes and serve with the turkey.

5 Heat the oven to 350°F. Melt the shortening in a large ovenproof dish on top of the stove. Fry the turkey in the shortening until it is brown all over. Roast the turkey, breast side down, in the oven for at least 2 hours. Turn it over as soon as it starts to look brown. From time to time, spoon over some roasting juices.

let's make...
HOPPIN' JOHN

In the South, we always eat "Hoppin' John" for New Year's Day, usually with mustard greens. It is a good luck dish because the beans stand for coins and the greens for paper money.

WHAT YOU NEED:

SERVES 4 PEOPLE:

7 ounces dried blackeye
   beans
5 cups water
9 ounces smoked bacon
1 tablespoon cooking oil
1 large onion
1 garlic clove
1 cup long-grain rice
salt, black pepper
a few drops of
   Tabasco sauce

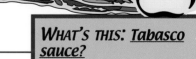

◁ Sometimes Mom puts a coin into the meal. It is said that whoever finds the coin will be lucky in the coming year. But I think we can all be happy anyway, if we try hard enough.

WHAT'S THIS: *Tabasco sauce?*

Tabasco is a pepper sauce made on Avery Island in Louisiana. It was first made in 1868, and has become famous around the world. Fresh peppers are picked and mashed. Then they are sealed in oak barrels to mature for three years. You can use any other hot sauce instead.

1 Wash the beans in a sieve under cold water. Put the beans into a large saucepan, add 5 cups cold water, and leave to soak overnight.

2 The following day, bring the water to a boil, cover the saucepan, and cook for about 1 hour. **!**

4 Add the onion and fry until it is transparent (see-through). Peel the garlic and crush it into the skillet. Stir, then take the skillet off the heat.

3 Meanwhile, chop the bacon into small cubes. Peel and chop the onion *(see page 5)*. Put the bacon and the oil in a skillet, heat, and fry until the bacon is crisp. **!**

5 Add the bacon–onion mixture and the rice to the beans. Cover and simmer for about 20 minutes, until the rice and the beans are cooked. If it all looks too dry or starts to stick to the pan, add a little more water. Season generously with salt, pepper, and Tabasco. Serve hot. **!**

How we celebrate at home in the
UNITED STATES

A part from the national, regional, and local festivities, there are also many occasions when families celebrate at home and in private. Many people in the United States are Christian, so many families celebrate the Christian holidays.

Christmas

Many Christmas traditions were brought to America by early settlers from Europe. Each region now has its own way of celebrating— partly because of the people who live in that region and partly due to varying climates. In California, for example, Santa Claus arrives by surfboard and in Hawaii by boat!

Many customs celebrate the Nativity story. People build cribs, or they re-enact the story of Joseph and Mary, for example. In Arizona, a huge bright star is lit on a mountain top. It can be seen for miles around—just like the star in the Bible. Before Christmas, carol singers go from house to house— this custom is originally from England.

Families celebrate Christmas together. In the German tradition, they put up a Christmas tree. The tree is hung with tinsel, colorful ornaments, and electric lights.

Some people go to midnight mass on Christmas Eve. They exchange gifts and presents on Christmas Day, December 25th.

The town of Santa Claus, Indiana, gets some three million letters from children each year. They are all answered here.

The story that is told to little children is that Santa Claus arrives during the night. He comes on a sled pulled by reindeer (caribou), and climbs down the chimney with a sack full of gifts. The Santa Claus story is a blend of different tales mostly from European countries.

On Christmas Day, families eat a festive dinner together. In most homes this is roast turkey, but in some regions other dishes are prepared. In Virginia, for example, oyster and ham pie is the dish of the day. In the Southern States, people often have hominy grits soufflé and fruit cake together.

Christmas lights are an important tradition. They can be seen in store windows and in the streets. They celebrate not only the birth of Christ, but also the return of light after darkness on December 21st—the shortest day of the year. Many other countries and religions also have lights at this time of year.

◁ *Christmas lights* can be quite spectacular, made up of hundreds of thousands of lights. Neighbors compete for who has the biggest and best display of trees, Santas, reindeer, sleds, and gifts.

Birthday parties

Many children celebrate their birthday with a party. They receive presents from their family and friends. The birthday cake often carries the same number of candles as the child will be in years. Everyone sings "Happy Birthday" as the birthday child makes a silent wish and blows out all the candles in one breath.

The birthday cake may be a novelty cake with a personal message. It may show the name of the birthday person. Other cakes show something that relates to that person's hobbies, interests, or job. They may show a tennis court, for example, if the person enjoys playing tennis.

Sweet Sixteen

The sixteenth birthday is often a special day. It is the age when young people are believed to have reached maturity. They often have great parties. Jewish girls are thought to be grown up when they are twelve *(bat mitzvah)*, Jewish boys when they are thirteen *(bar*

△ *A cookoff* is often part of a family celebration. People cook chili or they barbecue meat. Crawfish are boiled in Louisiana. The cookoff can be a serious competition or just family fun.

mitzvah). The *bar mitzvah* and *bat mitzvah* are religious observances and so Jewish girls often celebrate the Sweet Sixteen as well.

Halloween

Halloween is celebrated on October 31st. The word comes from All Hallows' Eve, the evening before All Saints Day, which is on November 1st.

Children dress up in spooky costumes such as witches and wizards. They go from house to house to "trick-or-treat." Usually they get candies from people who don't want to have a trick played on them. Another custom on this day is to carve a face out of a hollow pumpkin called a jack-o-lantern. A candle is placed inside to make the face grin—or growl.

◁ **For Halloween** this girl is wearing a witch costume. Other favorite costumes include vampires, ghosts, or pumpkins. The more creative the idea, the better.

let's make...
SPARE RIBS

We cook spare ribs on Independence Day, when we invite our friends around for a big barbecue party. We also have burgers, hot dogs, steaks, and plenty of lemonade and ice cream.

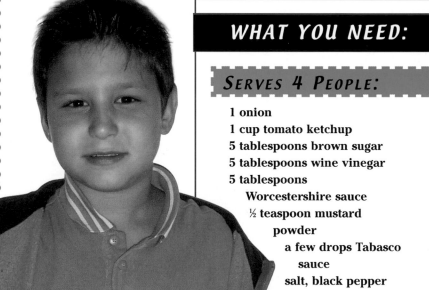

WHAT YOU NEED:

SERVES 4 PEOPLE:

1 onion
1 cup tomato ketchup
5 tablespoons brown sugar
5 tablespoons wine vinegar
5 tablespoons
  Worcestershire sauce
½ teaspoon mustard
  powder
    a few drops Tabasco
      sauce
    salt, black pepper
3–4 lbs spare ribs
  (pork rib,
    separated into
    individual ribs)

◁ I put plenty of ketchup on my spare ribs. It makes them turn black, but I like that smoky flavor.

WHAT'S THIS:
Worcestershire sauce?

This spicy sauce, or condiment, is also known as Worcester sauce. It comes originally from England and has many "secret" ingredients. These may include: soy sauce, vinegar, molasses sugar, garlic, tamarind, anchovies, scallions, and many other flavorings.

1 Peel and finely chop the onion *(see page 5)*. Put the onion into a saucepan with the ketchup, 5 tablespoons water, sugar, vinegar, Worcestershire sauce, mustard powder, and the Tabasco sauce. **!**

2 Season the sauce with salt and pepper. Bring it to a boil, stirring all the time. Reduce the heat. Simmer the sauce for about 5 minutes, stirring all the time, until the onion is soft.

3 Heat the oven to 400°F. Wash the spare ribs under cold water and pat them dry. Brush the ribs thinly with some of the prepared sauce.

4 Place the ribs side by side on a baking tray, with the meaty side at the top. Cook the ribs in the oven for 45–60 minutes, depending on how thick they are. Turn the ribs a few times and brush with some more sauce. Add a little water in the baking tray if the juices start to look very dark. **!**

HOW DO I COOK SPARE RIBS ON THE <u>barbecue?</u>

Heat the grill. Place the ribs on a grid that is not too close to the charcoal. This ensures that they cook slowly. Grill for 45–60 minutes, depending on how thick the ribs are. Turn them a few times, and brush with more sauce.

let's make...
HAMBURGERS

This really is our national dish! While the hamburger may originally have come from Hamburg, Germany, we have made it our all-American top favorite.

WHAT YOU NEED:

MAKES 4 BURGERS:

1½ lbs beef (choose beef from the shoulder or the leg)
salt, black pepper
4 burger buns (wholegrain or sesame baps)

toppings of your choice:
ketchup, mayo, mustard, onion rings, cucumber slices, dill pickles, tomato slices, lettuce leaves

◁ Eating lots of high-calorie, fatty burgers is not good for you. But a homemade one, once in a while, is truly delicious!

1 Heat the grill. Trim the beef. If the meat is very fatty, cut some off—but some fat should stay on the meat.

2 Push the meat through a meat grinder. Don't set it too fine: very finely ground meat makes dry burgers. **!**

3 Season the ground beef with salt and pepper.

5 Place the burgers on the BBQ (or put them in a skillet with a little oil). Grill (or fry) each side for about 3–4 minutes. This leaves the burgers nicely pink and juicy inside. **!**

6 Cut open the buns and toast them on the BBQ (or fry them briefly in a dry skillet). Assemble the burger with the toppings of your choice. **!**

4 Shape the meat into patties, just under 1 inch thick. Make the edges smooth and straight. Don't knead it for too long—this will make the burgers dry out.

How we live in the
UNITED STATES

T he United States is a mainly urban society. This means that more people live in the cities than in the countryside. The people who live in the United States come from many different ethnic backgrounds.

City life

The cities with the largest numbers of people are New York City (New York), Los Angeles (California), Chicago (Illinois), Houston (Texas), and Philadelphia (Pennsylvania). The states with the most people are California and Texas—ever more people are leaving the north and the east to move to these states.

As in other countries, the cities are the places with the most jobs, with more schools and universities, and many museums and theaters. They include areas of enormous wealth as well as extreme poverty. Great efforts are made to help disadvantaged people. But often it is the minority populations who experience the greatest poverty.

Leisure

The United States is a great sporting nation. At the Olympic Games and other international competitions, American athletes often win the most medals. The No. 1 favorite sport is baseball, followed by American football and basketball. Ice hockey and soccer are also popular.

Life at school

Most children go to public elementary (or grade) and secondary schools (often known as middle school and high school). Some children go to private schools where the parents have to pay for their education. Private schools are often religious schools. Children have to go to school until the age of sixteen, and in some states until eighteen. After secondary school, some students will go on to earn a degree at a college or university.

Time off

Many Americans love outdoor activities. If the parents can afford it, children stay at a summer camp during their vacation. There they may learn horseback riding, sailing, canoeing, and woodcraft, as well as tennis and archery.

◁ **American football** is also known as "football." The championship game of the National Football League is the Super Bowl. More than half of all Americans watch it on TV. The players are often spurred on by cheerleaders, who perform amazing dance and acrobatic routines.

They go camping, hiking, fishing, and climbing, and they have lots of picnics and barbecues. In summer, white-water rafting is a popular sport, and in winter, back-country skiing and snowboarding.

Country life

Fewer people than ever work on farms in the United States. This is partly because farms have become very "successful": they use fertilizers and water their plants artificially to make them grow better, and they use pesticides to protect them from bugs. But there are also fewer jobs because it is often cheaper to import food from other countries than to grow it at home. Instead, many people in the country now work in the

▽ *Cowboys and farmhands* still drive cattle to market. They also feed and brand the cows they look after. They check the fencing and the water supply on the range. They move cows to different areas to graze. Some also perform at rodeos.

service industries. They look after tourists or manage the land; they work for insurance and real estate offices, at stores, or dry cleaners. Some work in computing.

Family life

As in other western countries, American children and other family members spend long hours every day watching TV programs or using the computer. They play games or visit Internet chatrooms. Only one-third of families now make dinners from scratch. Mostly, people have fast-food or take-out meals, often not eaten at the family table.

Unfortunately, lack of exercise and bad food have made many children and young people in the United States overweight, or obese. And this can lead to bad health.

△ **Native Americans** lived in the United States long before Europeans settled there. They belong to many different tribes and states, and have won the right to govern themselves.

let's make...
PANCAKES & MAPLE SYRUP

This is the best breakfast dish in the world. It helps me get out of bed when I'm still tired. If I can smell pancakes from the kitchen, I'll be up, washed and ready in no time at all.

WHAT YOU NEED:

SERVES 4 PEOPLE:

1 cup wheat flour
1 teaspoon baking powder
1 teaspoon maple syrup
a pinch of salt
1 large egg
½ cup buttermilk
butter for frying
maple syrup for drizzling

◁ I love these pancakes with fruit and maple syrup. Try them with apples or blueberries as well.

WHAT'S THIS: maple syrup?

This syrup is made from the sap of maple trees. It comes mainly from the northeastern states and Canada. Look for the maple leaf.

MY TIP

Dot the pancakes with butter, and serve them with some crispy fried bacon as well as the syrup.

1 Stir together the flour, baking powder, maple syrup, salt, egg, and buttermilk to make a smooth batter. Allow the batter to rest and swell for about 30 minutes.

2 Melt a little butter in a nonstick skillet. Add a ladleful of the batter and smooth it slightly with the back of the ladle. Fry for about 2 minutes. **!**

4 Take out of the pan and keep warm in a low oven (200°F). Continue frying more ladles of batter in the skillet until you have about 12 small, round pancakes. **!**

3 Turn the pancake over and fry for another 3–4 minutes or until golden brown on both sides.

5 To serve, drizzle the pancakes with plenty of maple syrup.

let's make...
CHILI CON CARNE

This is *not* a Mexican dish but the official dish of Texas! There are hundreds of different recipes, and people can get quite heated about which to use. We even hold chili "cookoffs."

WHAT YOU NEED:

SERVES 4 PEOPLE:

2½ lbs beef (shoulder or ribsteak)
1 large onion
5–6 fresh red chilies
4 garlic cloves
5 tablespoons cooking oil
1 cup beef stock
1 teaspoon brown sugar
1 bay leaf
2 teaspoons dried thyme
salt

½ teaspoon ground cumin
Cayenne pepper
1 tablespoon Worcestershire sauce
2–3 teaspoons fine corn flour

◁ If the chili becomes too spicy, just drink a glass of milk to cool your mouth.

POPULAR TYPES OF *chili pepper*:

• Anaheim—very mild; large, deep, shiny green. Often stuffed or added to salsas. • Cayenne—hot; long, skinny, and wrinkled; deep green, yellow, orange, or red. • Jalapeno—hot; dark green to red. • Poblano—mild to medium; dark green, shiny, and large. • Serrano—fairly hot; used in Thai or Mexican dishes.

1 Wash the beef and pat it dry. Cut it into very small cubes. Cut out and throw away any large pieces of fat. Peel and finely chop the onion. Wash, trim, and deseed the chilies, then cut them into thin rings (see page 5). Peel and crush the garlic.

2 Heat the oil in a large, heavy saucepan. Add the beef cubes and the onion, a handful at a time. Fry and stir, but don't let them get too dark. Stir in the chilies and the garlic.

3 Pour in the stock. Season with sugar, bay leaf, thyme, salt, cumin, Cayenne pepper, and Worcestershire sauce. Stir everything, then cover the saucepan and simmer over very low heat for about 1½ hours. Stir from time to time and add more water if the chili looks too dry.

4 Just before serving, stir in the corn flour to thicken the chili a little. Heat through. Garnish with grated cheese, sour cream, or chopped tomato. Serve with cornbread or corn chips.

let's make...
CHOCOLATE FUDGE

Mom says this fudge is a great thing to have around the house when guests drop in unexpectedly. And it also makes a tasty gift; for example, when you're going to a potluck dinner.

▽ Why doesn't my Mom want me to eat fudge? I have no idea!

WHAT YOU NEED:

MAKES 28 PIECES:

2 cups powdered sugar
¼ cup unsweetened cocoa powder
½ cup butter
5 tablespoons milk
⅓ cup pecans or walnuts (optional)
½ teaspoon vanilla essence

MY TIP

You can make this fudge extra-delicious by toasting the nuts first. Preheat the oven to 350°F and place the nuts on a rack in the center of the oven for about 8 minutes, or until they are light brown and fragrant. Cool and then chop them coarsely.

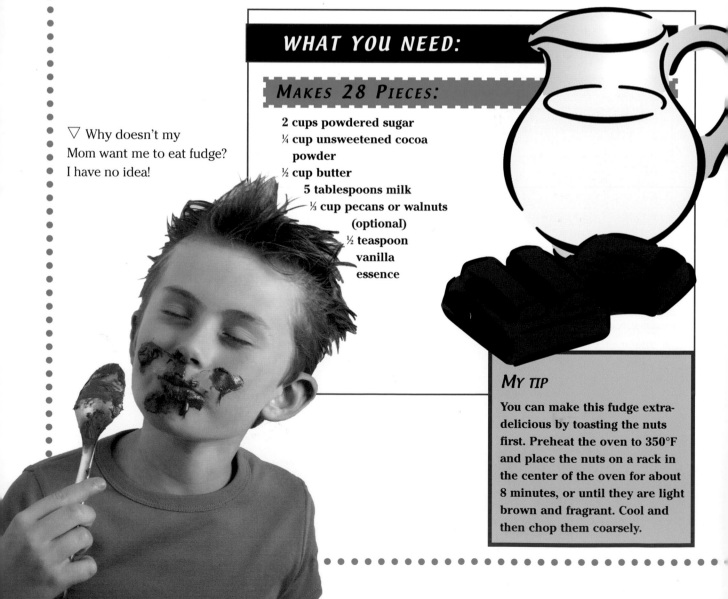

1 Sift the powdered sugar and the cocoa powder through a sieve into a saucepan. Thoroughly grease an 8-inch-long rectangular baking pan.

2 Put the rest of the butter and the milk into the saucepan. Bring the mixture to a boil, stirring all the time. Reduce the heat and simmer over a low heat for about 20 minutes. Stir all the time so the mixture doesn't burn. **!**

4 Add the chocolate mixture and smooth the top. Place the mold on a rack and allow it to cool and set.

3 Finely chop the nuts and stir them into the chocolate mixture together with the vanilla essence. **!**

5 Tip the fudge out of the mold onto a board. Cut the fudge into small squares. Wrap the fudge well in plastic wrap or aluminum foil so the pieces do not dry out.

Look it up
UNITED STATES

breadbasket the name given to the plains area where most of the corn and cereals are grown in the United States

chili con carne a famous Texan beef stew, often spicy

cookoff a cooking competition, often for cooking chili con carne

Halloween October 31st, the evening before All Hallows

Hispanics Spanish-speaking people in the United States and elsewhere

Hoppin' John a Southern New Year's Day dish made from blackeye beans; it is supposed to bring good luck

Jambalaya a Southern one-pot rice dish, often made with meat or seafood

key limes small, round, pale yellow limes, named after Key West in Florida and used in key lime pie

krewe a carnival association in New Orleans; krewes organize parades and elect a "king;" they also sponsor dances.

Latinos Spanish-speaking people from Latin America, that is from Central or South America

longhorn a famous breed of Texan cattle with long horns

Mardi Gras from French "fat Tuesday," the day before Ash Wednesday and the start of fasting; the climax of carnival celebrations in New Orleans

ranch a large farm in the western United States where herds of cattle, sheep, or horses are raised

range the open, public land where cattle are allowed to graze and roam freely

St. Patrick's Day a holiday for the Irish community, celebrating the life of a Catholic saint and Irish traditions

Find out more
UNITED STATES

Books to read

D'Amico, Joan, and Drummond, Karen Eich. **The United States Cookbook: Fabulous Foods and Fascinating Facts from 50 States.**
Jossey-Bass: 2000.

Kalman, Bobbie, and Calder, Kate. **United States from A to Z.**
Crabtree Publishing: 1998.

Miller, Millie, and Nelson, Cyndi. **State-by-State Guide: United States of America.**
Scholastic Reference: 2006.

National Geographic United States Atlas for Young Explorers
National Geographic Children's Books: 2004.

Web sites to check out

www.kids.gov
Official children's portal for the U.S. government. Links and sites grouped by age and subject

www.usa.gov
The government's official web site, with downloadable documents such as the Declaration of Independence

www3.nationalgeographic.com/places/countries/country_unitedstates.html
National Geographic's site about the United States, with information about history, travel, and flags, and photographs

www.factmonster.com/us.html
Lots of facts—history, law, education, landmarks, ethnicity, and so on

www.mypyramid.gov/kids
Interactive games, tips, and worksheets from the U.S. Department of Agriculture

Index
UNITED STATES